SETTLERS *and* Invaders *of Britain*

The Celts, Picts, Scots and Romans

Ben Hubbard

raintree

a Capstone company — publishers for children

Raintree is an imprint of Capstone Global Library Limited, a company incorporated in England and Wales having its registered office at 264 Banbury Road, Oxford, OX2 7DY – Registered company number: 6695582

www.raintree.co.uk
myorders@raintree.co.uk

Edited by Helen Cox Cannons
Designed by Cynthia Della-Rovere
Original illustrations © Capstone Global Library Limited 2018
Picture research by Tracy Cummins
Production by Kathy McColley
Originated by Capstone Global Library Limited
Printed and bound in India

ISBN 978 1 4747 5501 6 (hardback)
22 21 20 19 18
10 9 8 7 6 5 4 3 2 1

ISBN 978 1 4747 5505 4 (paperback)
23 22 21 20 19
10 9 8 7 6 5 4 3 2 1

British Library Cataloguing in Publication Data
A full catalogue record for this book is available from the British Library.

Acknowledgements
We would like to thank the following for permission to reproduce photographs: Alamy: Angelo Hornak, 13, David Lyons, 19, Heritage Image Partnership Ltd, 9; Bridgeman Images: Corbridge Roman Town Museum (Hadrian's Wall), Corbridge, UK / © Historic England, 25, Private Collection/© Look and Learn, 28; Capstone: Eric Gohl, 8, 15; Captone: Beehive Illustration/Martin Sanders, 5; Getty Images: Heritage Images, 10, Windmill Books, 26; iStockphoto: Gannet77, 27; Newscom: Ann Ronan Picture Library Heritage Images, 14, English Heritage Images, 11; Shutterstock: abxyz, 22, Andrew McLean, 17, Bill McKelvie, 18, Cat Design, Design Element, Claudio Divizia, 24, Combatcamerauk, 29, cosma, 7 Middle, David Peter Robinson, 12, gabriel12, Design Element, image4stock, Design Element, jps, 6 Top, Kraft_Stoff, 20, OgnjenO, 4, Panptys, Design Element, Peter Hermes Furian, 21, Pushkin, Design Element, ReVelStockArt, Design Element, S Buwert, Design Element, Stamatoyoshi, Cover, 1, SueC, 23, TTphoto, 16.

We would like to thank Dr Stephen Bowman, Lecturer in History at the University of the Highlands and Islands, for his invaluable help in the preparation of this book.

CONTENTS

Some words in this book appear in bold, **like this**. You can find out what they mean by looking in the glossary.

ANCIENT BRITAIN

The **Iron Age** was a period of great change in Britain. The discovery of iron in the 800s BC led to better tools for farming and stronger weapons for fighting. At this time, Britain was a violent and uncertain place. It was made up of **tribes** who often attacked and invaded each other's **settlements**. There were lots of different groups of peoples, including groups we now know as the Celts, Picts and Scoti.

A settled island

The Celts, Picts and Scoti were not the first people to live in Britain: people had lived there for more than 800,000 years before them. During the **Stone Age**, people had learned to grow crops, keep animals and build Britain's first permanent settlements. The Stone Age was followed by the **Bronze Age**. Bronze was a precious metal used to make tools, weapons and jewellery. People travelled to Britain to **trade** in bronze and the country became known about as far away as Greece and Rome.

The Celts fought with bronze weapons, such as this dagger. The holes show where the handle was attached to the blade.

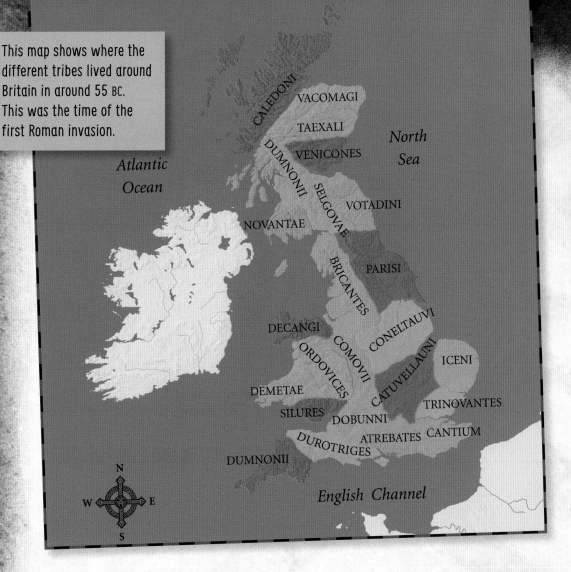

This map shows where the different tribes lived around Britain in around 55 BC. This was the time of the first Roman invasion.

CALEDONI
VACOMAGI
TAEXALI
VENICONES
DUMNONII
SELGOVAE
VOTADINI
NOVANTAE
BRICANTES
PARISI
DECANGI
CONELTAUVI
COMOVII
ORDOVICES
CATUVELLAUNI
ICENI
DEMETAE
SILURES
DOBUNNI
TRINOVANTES
DUROTRIGES
ATREBATES
CANTIUM
DUMNONII

Atlantic Ocean

North Sea

English Channel

N
W E
S

War and invasion

In the late Bronze Age, the population of Britain grew and people began to fight over land. Families joined together to form tribes and built large **fortified** settlements that could be defended against attack. During the Iron Age, many tribes went to war with each other. There were also attacks from abroad. Finally, as the Iron Age ended, Britain was invaded by the greatest power of the ancient world: the Romans. This is the story of the settlers and invaders who made up Britain's early history during those periods in time.

TIMELINE

Here is a timeline of all the events in the book. You can learn more about them as you read.

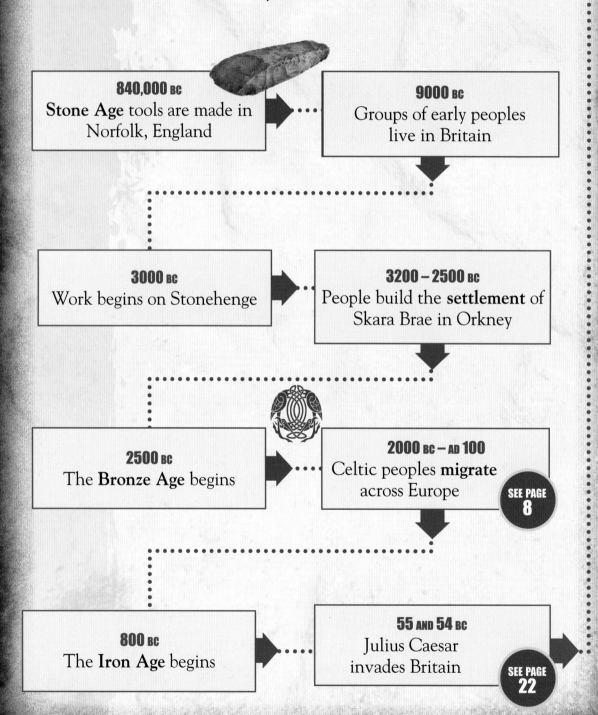

840,000 BC
Stone Age tools are made in Norfolk, England

9000 BC
Groups of early peoples live in Britain

3000 BC
Work begins on Stonehenge

3200 – 2500 BC
People build the **settlement** of Skara Brae in Orkney

2500 BC
The **Bronze Age** begins

2000 BC – AD 100
Celtic peoples **migrate** across Europe

SEE PAGE 8

800 BC
The **Iron Age** begins

55 AND 54 BC
Julius Caesar invades Britain

SEE PAGE 22

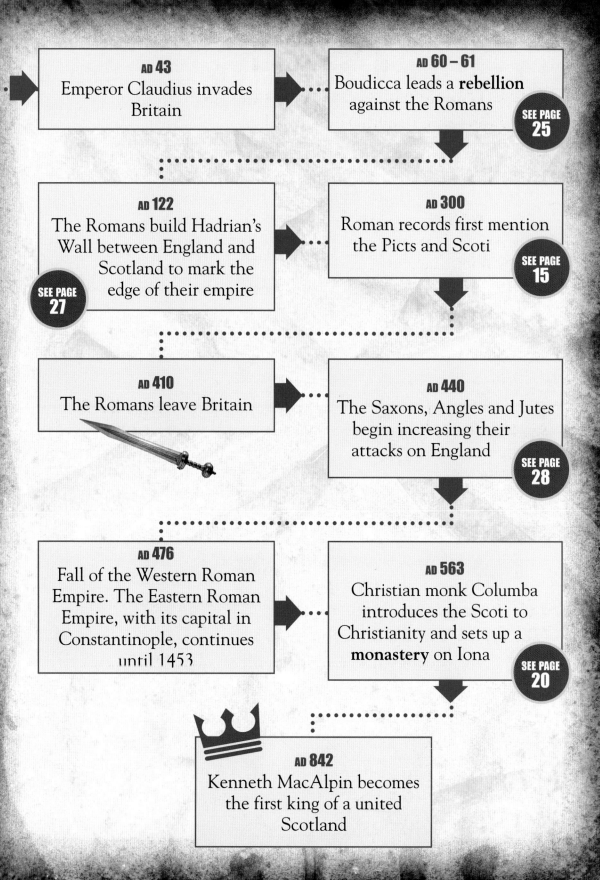

AD 43
Emperor Claudius invades Britain

AD 60–61
Boudicca leads a **rebellion** against the Romans

SEE PAGE
25

AD 122
The Romans build Hadrian's Wall between England and Scotland to mark the edge of their empire

SEE PAGE
27

AD 300
Roman records first mention the Picts and Scoti

SEE PAGE
15

AD 410
The Romans leave Britain

AD 440
The Saxons, Angles and Jutes begin increasing their attacks on England

SEE PAGE
28

AD 476
Fall of the Western Roman Empire. The Eastern Roman Empire, with its capital in Constantinople, continues until 1453

AD 563
Christian monk Columba introduces the Scoti to Christianity and sets up a **monastery** on Iona

SEE PAGE
20

AD 842
Kenneth MacAlpin becomes the first king of a united Scotland

THE CELTS

The Celts were a tribal people who **inhabited** many parts of Europe between 2000 BC and AD 100. They were not one united group, but were made up of many different **tribes**. These tribes seem to have shared a similar language, **culture** and beliefs.

Celtic peoples in Europe
around 250 BC

Celtic lands

Roman lands

Britons

Belgae

Hallstaft territory

Helvetii

Eastern Celts

Gauls

Hispano Celts

Roman Republic

Galatians

This map shows how much land the Celtic peoples inhabited in around 250 BC.

This 1st Century AD coin was made by the Catuvellauni tribe. Its chief, Cunobelinus, ruled over a large area north of the River Thames.

Why did the Celts come to Britain?

During the **Bronze Age** and **Iron Age**, waves of Celtic people moved across Europe in great **migrations**. Some tribes travelled to Britain to settle. Britain was a desirable country with fertile farmland and resources such as tin and copper to make bronze. Some of the Celtic tribes arriving in Britain probably took land by force, while others may have settled peacefully. The tribes already living in Britain were also influenced by the Celts. During the Iron Age, Celtic language, artworks and beliefs became the main culture of Britain. That is why we often call the Britons of this time Celts.

How life changed

An important Celtic influence was the introduction of new tools and farming techniques. These included the iron plough, which could dig quickly through fields of heavy soil. New varieties of crops, such as barley and wheat, were introduced that were easier to grow. There was now an **abundance** of food, and the population in Britain boomed. It reached more than one million people during the Iron Age.

Celtic warriors

The Celts were fearsome warriors who sometimes fought naked as a sign of bravery. Sometimes they painted themselves blue to look fierce. The Celts armed themselves with iron swords and helmets and chanted before battle. Celtic women would fight as well as men, and both men and women wore their hair long. They also decorated themselves with heavy bracelets and necklaces of gold and bronze.

Charging chariots

Some Celts rode into battle on board two-horse war-chariots. A charioteer would control the horses with reins, while a warrior beside him would hurl spears at the enemy. Once the chariot was close to the enemy lines, the warrior would jump out to fight hand-to-hand. The chariot would then retreat, so another chariot could ride in.

The Romans described the speed and skill of the charioteers. The charioteers would drive up and down battle lines and the noise and speed would threaten the Roman soldiers.

Danebury hill fort was built around 2,500 years ago. Around 300–400 people lived there for more than 400 years.

Iron Age fighting

By the middle of the Iron Age there was regular fighting between the **tribes** in Britain. At the Danebury **hill fort** near Hampshire, a pit full of human bones with battle injuries was found by archaeologists during the 1900s. These bones almost certainly belonged to the warriors of Danebury and the other three hill forts in the area. Celtic tribes often lived close to each other and fought over land. Some chieftains would also fight their neighbours for valuable possessions such as horses, and to settle **disputes**.

How Do We Know?

The Romans who fought the Celts recorded descriptions about the warriors. General Julius Caesar invaded Britain and wrote about the Celtic war chariots in his writings called The Gallic War (58-49 BC). This is how we know about their use in battle.

Celtic tribes

Celtic **tribes** were made up of chieftains, Druids, nobles, freemen and slaves. At the top were the chieftains, the most powerful men in Iron Age Britain. The chieftains would listen closely to their Druids. Druids were priests and priestesses who would advise on social and religious matters. The freemen in the tribe took orders from the chieftain and were responsible for fighting when the time came.

Roundhouses and forts

Many Celts lived in roundhouses with thatched roofs. Inside, the people shared one open room, often with their farm animals. Large tribes lived in roundhouses grouped together inside **hill forts**. A hill fort was surrounded by defensive ditches, earth banks and wooden fences called palisades. Other buildings inside hill forts included food stores, workshops and religious halls. Hill forts could be seen for miles around and were a symbol of a tribe's power and status.

A Celtic roundhouse had a cone-shaped roof. Inside there was a fireplace in the centre for light, warmth and to cook on.

Maiden Castle in Dorset was a great Celtic hill fort abandoned in the 1st Century AD after the Roman conquest. You can still see its ditches and banks today.

Celtic customs

When a tribe was not at war, daily life revolved around farming, preparing food, craftwork and making clothes. Celtic clothes included long shirts and baggy trousers for men. Women wore long dresses. Both men and women wore cloaks, held in place with a brooch. At night, food such as meat stews and flatbreads were prepared and children were entertained with stories and songs, sometimes told by **bards**. This is how Celtic history, customs and myths were explained to children. Children were also expected to help their parents carry out all the daily jobs, so they could follow in their parents' footsteps as adults.

Celtic beliefs

The Celts believed in many gods and goddesses and made **offerings** to keep them happy. Making an offering meant throwing valuable items, such as swords, shields and silver cauldrons, into sacred places, including rivers and lakes. It was hoped that offerings and **sacrifices** would encourage the gods to protect the tribe and provide them with enough food.

The Gundestrup cauldron is a famous Celtic bowl. It is made of silver.

Mistletoe and magic

The Druids acted as the tribe's doctors and treated people by performing magic rituals and creating cures from plants. Some cures were herbs and plants mixed together and drunk as a tea. A popular plant with Druids was mistletoe, which they believed had magical properties.

THE PICTS AND SCOTI

The Picts and the Scoti were the two **Iron Age** groups of **peoples** who shared what is now Scotland. The Picts were known as "Picti" or "painted people" by the Romans. This was probably because of the tattoos or warpaint the Picts used to decorate their bodies. The Scoti were seafaring peoples from Ireland who settled in Scotland.

This map shows where in Britain the Picts and Scoti lived in around AD 300.

Picts

Scoti

Britons

Pict and Scoti tribes

The Picts and Scoti often behaved like their neighbours to the south. Sometimes they attacked each other and at other times they joined forces to fight a common enemy. The Picts lived in the north and east of Scotland, which they called Pictland. The Scoti lived in the west, which they called Dál Riada. Separating the two **tribes** was the vast Grampian mountain range. This meant the Picts and Scoti were kept apart and developed different forms of language and **culture**.

Mousa Broch is an Iron Age roundhouse on the Shetland islands. It is believed to have been built in around 300 BC.

This reconstruction of a Crannog is at Loch Tay. It shows what crannogs would have looked like.

Different dwellings

Both the Pict and Scoti tribes lived in similar roundhouses to those built by the Celts. They also constructed stone towers called brochs, with walls up to four metres thick. Crannogs were another type of Iron Age dwelling built in Scotland during this time. A crannog was a roundhouse built on a platform in a lake. Each crannog was connected to the shore by a long, narrow ramp, which made it easy to defend.

How Do We Know?

The Picts and the Scoti did not keep written records about themselves. Most of what we know about these groups of peoples comes from archaeology and what was written about them by the Romans. We also have written records about tribes from Christian monks.

On this rocky land in Argyll once stood the Scoti hill fort of Dunadd. Between about AD 500 and 900 it was the capital of the kingdom.

Pict and Scoti life

One clue into the life of the Picts comes from their symbol stones, many of which remain standing today. Each stone was ornately carved, often with mysterious symbols such as discs, crescents and swirling circles. Others were illustrated with images of animals such as salmon and horses. Fish and horses were of great importance to the Picts, who were skilled fishermen and horse riders.

The Scoti overking

The Scoti built a **hill fort** on a rocky crag called Dunadd in modern Argyll. From here, an overking ruled over clans called kindreds. Each kindred was given land to farm and paid tribute to the overking in return. Tributes often consisted of food, such as honey and sheep, which were used to feed the overking's warriors. The overking spent much of his time riding around Dál Riada making sure the kindreds paid their tributes. With the wealth created from these tributes, the overking held large feasts and bought ornate jewellery.

Scoti jewellery

Scoti craftsmen had many workshops around Dunadd where they made elaborate brooches, necklaces and rings. The moulds used to make this silver and gold jewellery are still being discovered today. A mould was an imprint carved in stone that hot metal was poured into to make a piece of jewellery. The king would keep the most impressive jewellery for himself, but sent other pieces to his nobles to reward their loyalty.

This is a copy of an ancient bird's head brooch that was found at Dunadd hill fort.

Pict and Scoti beliefs

Up until the AD 500s, the Picts and Scoti were **pagans**. Then, in AD 563, a group of monks led by a man called Columba brought Christianity to Dál Riada. The Scoti king gave Columba land on Iona to build a monastery. Meanwhile, a different form of Christianity was being set up in Northumbria, just south of Pictland. The Picts had to choose which type of Christianity to follow.

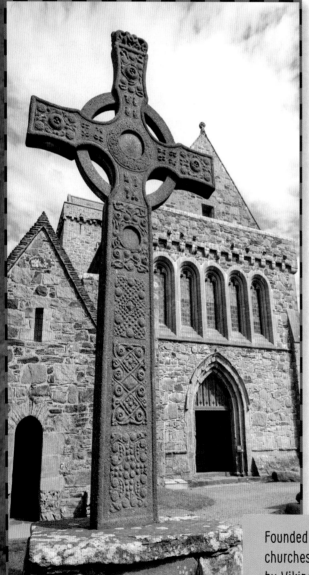

Religious differences

The Picts decided to adopt the Northumbrian form of Christianity, which took its orders directly from the Pope in Rome. As a result of this decision, relations broke down between the Picts and Scoti. The Picts invaded Dál Riada and took the Scoti capital at Dunadd. This might have been the end for the Scoti if a new common enemy had not appeared off the coast of Scotland: the Vikings. A new king called Kenneth MacAlpin then united the Picts and Scoti against the Vikings. Kenneth MacAlpin is today remembered as the first king of Scotland.

Founded in AD 563, Iona Abbey is one of the oldest churches in Scotland. It was attacked several times by Vikings in the 8th and 9th centuries.

THE ROMANS

During the **Iron Age**, the Romans became the greatest **conquerors** of the ancient world. Based in Italy, the Romans built an empire that stretched from the Middle East and North Africa across most of western Europe. In 55 BC, the Romans set out to invade Britain.

This map shows the Roman Empire at its largest, in around AD 117. It shows the huge area that the Romans conquered, from modern-day western Europe to the Middle East.

The Roman invasion

The Romans were on a mission to **conquer** and control the largest empire the world had ever known. They did this with a highly trained army. The Roman army used new battle formations to conquer less organized armies. Captured enemies were taken as slaves, used as gladiators, or made to promise loyalty to Rome. The great wealth taken from conquered lands made the Roman Empire rich and strong.

Why did the Romans come?

Britain had many resources that could help the Romans. These resources included tin, copper, gold, crops, cloth and slaves. Conquering Britain was also a challenge for the famous Roman general Julius Caesar, who wanted to prove his power in battle. In 55 BC, Caesar landed on the coast of Kent with 20,000 **legionaries** and 2,000 horses. He was beaten back by Celtic warriors who were waiting for him. In 54 BC, Caesar returned and defeated the Celts. The Celts had united to fight the Romans under one king, Cassivellaunus. After the Romans invaded Britain, the Celts kept attacking and Caesar decided to leave again.

It was the Roman emperor Claudius who ordered the successful invasion of Britain in AD 43.

Roman legionaries were feared around the world for their power and discipline.

Defeating the Celts

In AD 43 the Romans, led by the emperor Claudius, were back. They arrived with war elephants and an army of 40,000 legionaries. Riding out to meet them was a Celtic army led by the chieftain Caratacus. The Romans defeated Caratacus in battle and then conquered all the Celtic **hill forts** in the British south. After Caratacus's stronghold at Colchester was destroyed, eleven Celtic chieftains surrendered to the Romans. Caratacus was paraded through the streets of Rome in chains. Britain now belonged to the Romans.

The Roman Great Bath in the city of Bath (then called Aquae Sulis), still has hot water that comes from a natural spring. Visitors believed that the water had healing powers.

Life in Britain under Roman rule

Roman rule brought about great change for the people of Britain. New Roman towns were constructed with temples, amphitheatres, public baths and **aqueducts**. Straight, flat paved roads between the towns replaced the muddy tracks that had existed before. The Romans also spread their **culture**, language and laws. As long as the Celts didn't cause trouble, however, the Romans were happy to let them follow their own gods and customs.

How life changed

The Romans brought many modern improvements to life in Britain. Celtic country roundhouses were soon replaced with rectangular Roman villas. Clean water was supplied to the towns via aqueducts. Goods from around the Roman Empire, such as olive oil, wine, glass, perfumes and spices, could be bought in the forums, or town squares. Hot food could be bought from street stalls. Many Britons moved to the towns to enjoy these new luxuries.

Boudicca

When the Romans conquered Britain in 54 BC, many Celtic **tribes** accepted their rule. But others never stopped fighting back. The most famous Celtic **rebel** was a warrior queen called Boudicca. Boudicca and her Celtic army attacked and burned the cities of Colchester (Camulodunum) and London (Londinium). Boudicca was finally defeated by the Romans in AD 60 or 61.

Life for a Celtic child

Life for Celtic children changed under Roman rule. Rich boys were trained with weapons and taught to read and write in Latin. They also learned how to speak in public. This was to prepare them for important jobs in the army and government. Only the wealthiest girls had the chance to be educated and slaves and poor children did not receive any education at all.

This Roman board game was found at Housesteads, a Roman fort at Hadrian's Wall.

Clothes and status

You could tell a person's place in Roman Britain by the way they dressed. Slaves and ordinary people wore plain tunics, but the rich and powerful liked to display their wealth with expensive clothes. Over time, these clothes became a mix of Roman and Celtic styles. This meant white Roman togas and tunics were decorated with checked Celtic squares and coloured with yellows, blues and reds. Large decorative Celtic belt buckles and brooches were also worn.

Food and farming

As Roman towns in Britain grew, there was greater demand for food, so farming became big business. Farmers learned to produce more crops and travelled along the fast, Roman roads to sell their food at town forums.

The Romans built flat, paved roads across their empire. This meant that legionaries could march quickly from one place to the next. It also helped to **trade** goods across countries.

Hadrian's Wall was built on the orders of the emperor Hadrian (AD 76–138). It was built to keep out **tribes** who rebelled against the Romans and place a border at the northernmost point of the Empire.

Life for a Roman legionary

Life for a Roman **legionary** was tough. When not fighting, legionaries had to train with weapons for two hours a day, build new roads and complete a 42-kilometre (26-mile) run once a month. Many legionaries from Italy grumbled about the cold British climate. But army life could be a good one for British men. They received regular money, had the chance to travel, and were given a plot of land when they retired.

Hadrian's Wall

One of the harshest jobs for a Roman legionary was to be posted to a fort along Hadrian's Wall. The wall is over 118 kilometres (73 miles) long and runs from the west coast to east coast of Britain near the modern-day border between England and Scotland. The wall was built to keep out tribes of Picts and Scoti, but these tribes continued to attack the Romans.

The end of Roman rule

For 150 years after the revolt of Boudicca, the Romans ruled over a peaceful and prosperous Britain. There was trouble, however, back in Rome. Rome's rule was weakened by a series of **corrupt** emperors and it began to lose control of its empire. By the end of the AD 300s, Rome was in steady decline and its borders were falling to **barbarian** tribes such as the Germanic Visigoths.

Rome was attacked in AD 410 by a barbarian tribe called the Visigoths, led by their king, Alaric. The rest of the Roman Empire's lands also came under attack from tribal forces.

Defending Britain

Although Rome's power declined, Britain remained prosperous during the AD 300s. In AD 383, however, Roman **legionaries** began to be withdrawn to protect Rome's borders in Italy. By AD 406, there were not enough troops in Britain to prevent the increasing attacks by the Picts, Scoti, Anglo-Saxons and Jutes. The Britons were told they had to defend themselves. In AD 410, barbarians invaded Rome and soon afterwards the Roman Empire fell. Britain was left to fend for itself.

These people have dressed up to act in an Anglo-Saxon battle. After the Romans left, the Anglo-Saxons settled in Britain.

Under attack

Britain fell under increasing attack from the Germanic Anglo-Saxons and the Picts and Scoti who broke through Hadrian's Wall. Some Britons fought the raiders off, others hired Anglo-Saxon **mercenaries** (paid professional soldiers) to protect them. Nobody could stop the Anglo-Saxon hoards, however, and slowly they took control.

How life changed

After the Romans left Britain in AD 410, the cities were slowly abandoned. Many technologies, such as **aqueducts** and public baths, that had made life better were abandoned. There was no central government to control the country or keep records of its history. Life in Britain became increasingly unstable and violent during this time. However a new wave of tribes were starting to come over from northern Europe and began to settle. They later became known as the Anglo-Saxons. A new era in Britain began.

GLOSSARY

abundance plenty of something

aqueduct channel made for carrying water

barbarian name used by the Romans to describe peoples who were not part of their civilization

bard storyteller and singer who told stories about history and mythology

Bronze Age period in history that lasted between around 2500 BC and 800 BC

conquer take control of an area or country by force

corrupt someone who behaves dishonestly to get money, possessions or power

culture customs and beliefs of a group of people

dispute disagreement or argument about something

hill fort fort built on a hill with ditches and banks around it, lived in by Iron Age peoples

fortified defended against attack

inhabit live in a place

Iron Age period in history that lasted between around 800 BC and AD 43

legionary Roman soldier

migration movement of people from one country to another

offering something given to please a god or goddess

pagan person believing in many gods and goddesses, instead of only one god

rebellion organized fight against a ruler or ruling group

sacrifice kill a living thing as an offering to a god

settlement place where people make their homes

Stone Age period in history that lasted between around 4000 BC and 2500 BC

trade buying and selling goods

tribe group of people with the same language, beliefs and customs

Find out more

Books

The Roman Empire and its Impact on Britain (Early British History), Claire Throp, (Raintree, 2016)

Changes in Britain from the Stone Age to the Iron Age (Early British History), Claire Throp, (Raintree, 2016)

Life in the Stone Age, Bronze Age and Iron Age (A Child's History of Britain), Anita Ganeri (Raintree, 2014)

Life in Roman Britain (A Child's History of Britain), Anita Ganeri (Raintree, 2014)

Websites

www.bbc.co.uk/history/handsonhistory/ancient-britain.shtml
Learn more about ancient Britain on this BBC website.

www.bbc.co.uk/wales/celts
This website has animated stories to help you learn about the Celts.

www.yac-uk.org/timeline/ironage
Interested in archaeology? Try the Young Archaeologists' Club.

Places to visit

If you want to visit some of the places in this book, find out more at the following websites:

The National Trust in England, Wales and Northern Ireland
www.nationaltrust.org.uk

The National Trust in Scotland
www.nts.org.uk/Home

English Heritage
www.english-heritage.org.uk

The Roman Baths, Bath
www.romanbaths.co.uk

INDEX